contents

beef soup with ramen and mushrooms

8 dried shiitake mushrooms
2 tablespoons peanut oil
500g beef strips
4 green onions, sliced thinly
2 cloves garlic, crushed
1cm piece fresh ginger (5g), grated
1 litre (4 cups) beef stock
3 cups (750ml) water
1 tablespoon light soy sauce
2 tablespoons rice wine
180g ramen

Place mushrooms in small heatproof bowl, cover with boiling water; stand 20 minutes, drain. Discard stems; slice caps thinly.
Heat half of the oil in large saucepan; cook beef, in batches, until browned all over. Heat remaining oil in same pan; cook half of the onion with garlic and ginger, stirring, until onion softens.
Add stock, the water, sauce and wine; bring to a boil. Add mushrooms, beef and noodles; bring to a boil. Reduce heat; simmer, uncovered, about 5 minutes or until noodles are tender. Serve soup sprinkled with remaining onion.

serves 4
per serving 15.8g fat; 1805kJ (433 cal)

miso soup with pork and green beans

100g pork fillet, sliced thinly
8 green beans, cut into 2cm lengths
¼ cup (75g) red miso paste (karakuchi)
4cm piece fresh ginger (20g), grated
2 green onions, chopped finely

secondary dashi
10g dried kelp (konbu), chopped coarsely
20g large smoked dried bonito flakes (katsuobushi)
1½ litres (6 cups) cold water

Make secondary dashi.

Bring dashi to a boil in medium saucepan. Add pork and beans; return to a boil, then reduce heat; simmer, uncovered, 2 minutes.

Place miso in small bowl; gradually add 1 cup (250ml) of the hot dashi, stirring, until miso dissolves. Add to dashi in saucepan, stir to combine. Bring to a boil; remove from heat immediately.

Divide soup among serving bowls. Squeeze grated ginger between two spoons to extract 2 teaspoons of ginger juice; stir ½ teaspoon ginger juice into each bowl. Serve soup sprinkled with onion.

secondary dashi place kelp and half of the bonito flakes in large saucepan with the water; bring to a boil. Reduce heat; simmer, uncovered, about 15 minutes or until dashi reduces to 1 litre (4 cups). Add extra bonito flakes; bring to a boil. Remove from heat; strain.

serves 4
per serving 3.3g fat; 355kJ (85 cal)
tip don't overcook soup after miso is added or some of the delicate flavour will be lost.

5

spicy teriyaki tuna

¾ cup (180ml) japanese soy sauce
2 tablespoons honey
¼ cup (60ml) mirin
1 tablespoon wasabi paste
1 teaspoon sesame oil
300g sashimi tuna steak
2 tablespoons pink pickled ginger, sliced thinly

Combine sauce, honey, mirin, wasabi and oil in medium bowl; reserve
½ cup of marinade in small jug. Place tuna in bowl with remaining marinade;
turn tuna to coat in marinade. Cover; refrigerate 3 hours or overnight. Drain
tuna; discard marinade.
Cook tuna in heated oiled medium frying pan until browned both sides and
cooked as desired (do not overcook as tuna has a tendency to dry out).
Cut tuna into 24 similar-sized pieces (approximately 2cm each).
Place chinese spoons on serving platter. Place 1 piece of tuna on each
spoon; top with 1 teaspoon of the reserved marinade and a little ginger.

makes 24
per spoon 0.9g fat; 138kJ (33 cal)

gyoza with soy vinegar sauce

300g pork mince

2 tablespoons kecap manis

1 teaspoon sugar

1 tablespoon sake

1 egg, beaten lightly

2 teaspoons sesame oil

3 cups (240g) finely shredded chinese cabbage

4 green onions, sliced thinly

40 gyoza or gow gee wrappers

1 tablespoon vegetable oil

soy vinegar sauce

½ cup (125ml) light soy sauce

¼ cup (60ml) red wine vinegar

2 tablespoons white vinegar

2 tablespoons sweet chilli sauce

Combine pork, kecap manis, sugar, sake, egg, sesame oil, cabbage and onion in large bowl; refrigerate 1 hour.

Place one heaped teaspoon of the pork mixture in centre of one wrapper; brush one edge of wrapper with a little water. Pleat damp side of wrapper only; pinch both sides together to seal. Repeat with remaining pork mixture and wrappers.

Cover base of large frying pan with water; bring to a boil. Add dumplings, in batches; reduce heat, simmer, covered, 3 minutes. Using slotted spoon, remove dumplings from pan. Drain pan; dry thoroughly.

Heat vegetable oil in same pan; cook dumplings, in batches, unpleated side and base only, until golden brown.

Serve hot with soy vinegar sauce.

soy vinegar sauce combine ingredients in small bowl.

makes 40

per gyoza 1.4g fat; 139kJ (31 cal)

per tablespoon sauce 0.1g fat; 35kJ (8 cal)

sushi rice

1 cup (200g) koshihikari rice
1 cup (250ml) water

sushi vinegar
2 tablespoons rice vinegar
1 tablespoon sugar
¼ teaspoon salt

Place rice in large bowl, fill with cold water, stir with one hand; drain. Repeat process two or three times until water is almost clear. Drain rice in strainer 30 minutes.

Meanwhile, prepare sushi vinegar.

Place drained rice and the water in medium saucepan, cover tightly; bring to a boil, then reduce heat; simmer, covered tightly, on low heat about 12 minutes or until water is absorbed. Remove from heat; stand, covered, 10 minutes.

Spread rice in large non-metallic bowl. Using large flat wooden spoon or plastic spatula, repeatedly slice through rice at a sharp angle to break up lumps and separate grains, gradually pouring in sushi vinegar. Not all of the vinegar may be required; the rice shouldn't become wet.

Continue to lift and turn rice with spoon, from outside to centre of bowl, about 5 minutes or until rice is almost cool. Cover rice with damp cloth while making sushi variations of your choice.

sushi vinegar stir combined ingredients in small bowl until sugar dissolves.

makes 2 cups
per ¼ cup 0.1g fat; 35kJ (8 cal)
tip sushi rice can be made up to 4 hours ahead. Cover; refrigerate until required.

sushi handrolls *(temaki-zushi)*

10 sheets toasted seaweed (yaki-nori)
⅓ cup (100g) mayonnaise
1 teaspoon wasabi paste
2 cups prepared sushi rice (see page 10)
60g cooked crab, shredded
1 lebanese cucumber (130g), seeded, sliced thinly
1 small avocado (200g), sliced thinly
1 small red capsicum (150g), sliced thinly

Cut each sheet of seaweed into 4 squares. Combine mayonnaise and wasabi in small bowl.

Place a quarter-sheet of seaweed, shiny-side down, diagonally across palm of left hand. Dip fingers of right hand in bowl of vinegared water; shake off excess. Mould rounded teaspoons of rice into oblong shape; place across centre of seaweed. Wet fingers; gently rake rice evenly over seaweed, making a slight groove down the middle of the rice for filling. Swipe a dab of wasabi mayonnaise along the groove, then top with a little crab, cucumber, avocado and capsicum.

Fold one side of seaweed over; fold other side of seaweed over the first to form a cone. Tip of cone can be folded back to hold cone shape securely.

Serve immediately with soy sauce, if desired.

makes 40
per handroll 1.6g fat; 155kJ (37 cal)

inside-out rolls (ura-maki-zushi)

2 sheets toasted seaweed (yaki-nori), halved lengthways
4 cups prepared sushi rice (see page 10)
2 teaspoons seven-spice mix (shichimi togarashi)
2 teaspoons black sesame seeds
2 teaspoons white sesame seeds
1½ tablespoons wasabi paste
1 small avocado (200g), sliced thinly
200g sashimi salmon, cut into 1cm strips
¼ cup (60ml) japanese soy sauce

Place one half-sheet of seaweed lengthways across bamboo mat about
2cm from the edge of mat closest to you. Dip fingers of one hand in bowl of
vinegared water, shake off excess; pick up a quarter of the rice, press onto
seaweed then gently rake rice evenly to completely cover seaweed.
Sprinkle quarter of the seven-spice mix and quarter of combined sesame
seeds over rice then cover rice completely with plastic wrap. Carefully lift
mat, turn over so seaweed faces up; place back on bamboo mat about
2cm from edge. Swipe a dab of wasabi across centre of seaweed then top
with about a quarter of the avocado and salmon, making certain the filling
extends to ends of seaweed.
Starting with edge closest to you, pick up mat with thumb and index finger
of both hands; use remaining fingers to hold filling in place as you roll mat.
Roll forward, pressing gently but tightly, wrapping rice around filling.
Continue rolling forward to complete roll. Unroll mat; keep roll in plastic wrap.
Using a sharp knife, cut roll, still in plastic wrap, in half then each half into
quarters, wiping knife between each cut. Remove plastic wrap.
Serve immediately with remaining wasabi and sauce.

makes 32
per roll 1.8g fat; 297kJ (71 cal)

chicken donburi

4 dried shiitake mushrooms
½ teaspoon dashi powder
1 cup (250ml) boiling water
4 medium brown onions (600g), sliced thinly
1½ cups (300g) koshihikari rice
3 cups (750ml) cold water
¼ cup (60ml) soy sauce
2 tablespoons mirin
1 teaspoon white sugar
600g chicken breast fillets, chopped coarsely
4 eggs, beaten lightly
2 green onions, sliced thinly

Place mushrooms in small heatproof bowl, cover with boiling water, stand 20 minutes; drain. Discard stems; slice caps thinly.

Meanwhile, combine dashi with the boiling water in small jug.

Cook brown onion in heated lightly oiled large frying pan, stirring, about 10 minutes or until onion is browned lightly. Add half of the dashi mixture, then reduce heat; simmer, stirring occasionally, about 10 minutes or until softened. Transfer to medium bowl.

Bring rice and the cold water to a boil in large saucepan; reduce heat and simmer, covered tightly, on low heat, about 12 minutes. Remove from heat; stand, covered, 10 minutes.

Meanwhile, combine remaining dashi mixture with sauce, mirin and sugar in same frying pan; bring to a boil. Add chicken and mushroom; cook, covered, about 5 minutes or until chicken is cooked through.

Combine egg with cooked onion in bowl, pour over chicken mixture; cook, covered, over low heat, about 5 minutes or until egg just sets.

Divide rice among serving bowls; top with chicken mixture, sprinkle with green onion.

serves 4
per serving 9.4g fat; 2328kJ (557 cal)

fried noodles

250g dried wheat noodles
2 tablespoons peanut oil
500g pork fillets, sliced thinly
1 large brown onion (200g), sliced thinly
1 medium red capsicum (200g), sliced thinly
1 medium green capsicum (200g), sliced thinly
2 cups (140g) coarsely shredded chinese cabbage
¼ cup (60ml) tonkatsu sauce
¼ cup (60ml) sukiyaki sauce

Cook noodles in large saucepan of boiling water, uncovered, until just tender; drain. Rinse under cold water; drain.

Meanwhile, heat half of the oil in wok; stir-fry pork, in batches, until browned all over.

Heat remaining oil in wok; stir-fry onion until soft. Add capsicum; stir-fry until just tender.

Return pork to wok with noodles, cabbage and sauces; stir-fry until cabbage just wilts.

serves 4
per serving 12.8g fat; 1931kJ (462 cal)
tip you can also use soba, fresh hokkien or rice noodles in this recipe.

tempura udon

320g dried thick udon
1 litre (4 cups) primary dashi (see page 25)
½ cup (125ml) japanese soy sauce
½ cup (125ml) mirin
8 large uncooked prawns (400g)
vegetable oil, for deep-frying
¼ cup (35g) plain flour
¼ teaspoon seven-spice mix (shichimi togarashi)
2 green onions, chopped finely

tempura batter
½ cup (75g) plain flour
½ cup (75g) cornflour
1 teaspoon baking powder
1 cup (250ml) iced soda water

Cook noodles in large saucepan boiling water, uncovered, until just tender; drain. Bring dashi, sauce and mirin to a boil in medium saucepan, then reduce heat; simmer broth 10 minutes.
Meanwhile, make tempura batter.
Shell and devein prawns, leaving tails intact. Score underside of prawns to prevent curling during cooking.
Heat oil in small saucepan. Dip prawns, one at a time, in flour, shake off excess; dip in tempura batter, one at a time, draining excess. Deep-fry prawns in batches until browned lightly; drain on absorbent paper.
Just before serving, divide noodles among serving bowls, place two prawns on top of noodles, ladle broth over and sprinkle with seven-spice mix. Serve sprinkled with onion.
tempura batter combine flours, baking powder and soda water in medium bowl. Do not overmix; mixture should be lumpy.

serves 4
per serving 22.1g fat; 2629kJ (629 cal)

pork-filled bean-curd pouches

½ cup (100g) koshihikari rice
2 teaspoons peanut oil
2 green onions, sliced thinly
1 clove garlic, crushed
1cm piece fresh ginger (5g), grated
2 red thai chillies, seeded, chopped finely
350g pork mince
12 seasoned fried bean-curd skins
12 chives

sesame-lime dipping sauce
¼ cup (60ml) light soy sauce
2 tablespoons rice vinegar
1 teaspoon sugar
1 tablespoon lime juice
¼ teaspoon sesame oil

Make sesame-lime dipping sauce.
Cook rice in large saucepan of boiling water, uncovered, until just tender; drain.
Meanwhile, heat oil in medium frying pan; cook onion, garlic, ginger and chilli until onion softens. Add pork; cook, stirring, until changed in colour and cooked through. Add rice to pork mixture; toss to combine.
Carefully cut open a bean-curd skin on one side, gently pushing fingers into each corner to form pouch. Fill pouch with a twelfth of the pork mixture, pushing mixture into corners but being careful not to overfill or tear pouch.
Tie pouch with a chive to enclose filling. Repeat with remaining pork mixture, bean-curd skins and chives. Serve pouches with sesame-lime dipping sauce.
sesame-lime dipping sauce combine ingredients in small bowl.

serves 4*
per serving 13.1g fat; 1345kJ (336 cal)

deep-fried tofu in broth

(age-dashi dofu)

300g firm tofu
2 tablespoons cornflour
vegetable oil, for deep-frying
¾ cup (180ml) primary dashi (see page 25)
2 tablespoons japanese soy sauce
2 tablespoons mirin
2 tablespoons finely grated daikon
4cm piece fresh ginger (20g), grated
1 green onion, chopped finely
2 teaspoons smoked dried bonito flakes (katsuobushi)

Press tofu between two chopping boards with a weight on top, raise one end to assist draining; stand 25 minutes.
Cut tofu into eight even-sized pieces; pat dry between layers of absorbent paper. Toss in cornflour, shake away excess cornflour. Heat oil in medium saucepan; deep-fry tofu, in batches, until browned lightly. Drain on absorbent paper.
Combine dashi, sauce and mirin in small saucepan; bring to a boil.
Place two pieces of tofu in each serving bowl; divide daikon, ginger and onion among bowls, pour over dashi mixture. Top with bonito flakes.

serves 4
per serving 9.4g fat; 665kJ (159 cal)

teriyaki beef

½ cup (125ml) mirin
⅓ cup (80ml) light soy sauce
¼ cup (50g) firmly packed brown sugar
1 tablespoon sake
4cm piece (20g) fresh ginger, grated
1 clove garlic, crushed
1 teaspoon sesame oil
1 tablespoon sesame seeds
750g beef fillet, sliced thinly
300g fresh baby corn, halved
2 green onions, sliced thinly

Combine mirin, sauce, sugar, sake, ginger, garlic, oil and seeds in large bowl. Stir in beef and corn; stand 5 minutes.
Drain beef mixture over medium saucepan; reserve marinade.
Cook beef and corn, in batches, on heated oiled grill plate (or grill or barbecue) until browned all over and cooked as desired.
Meanwhile, bring marinade to a boil. Reduce heat; simmer, uncovered, 5 minutes.
Serve beef and corn drizzled with hot marinade; sprinkle with onion. Serve on steamed rice, if desired.

serves 4
per serving 12.7g fat;1819kJ (435 cal)

pork tonkatsu

4 pork butterfly steaks (800g)
2 tablespoons light soy sauce
2 tablespoons mirin
1 clove garlic, crushed
1 egg, beaten lightly
2 cups (200g) packaged japanese breadcrumbs
vegetable oil, for shallow-frying
2 tablespoons pink pickled ginger

tonkatsu sauce
1 tablespoon worcestershire sauce
⅓ cup (80ml) tomato sauce
1 teaspoon light soy sauce
2 tablespoons sake
1 teaspoon japanese mustard

Make tonkatsu sauce.
Using meat mallet, gently pound pork between sheets of plastic wrap until about 1cm thick.
Combine sauce, mirin and garlic in large bowl. Add pork; mix well. Dip pork in egg; coat with breadcrumbs.
Heat oil in large frying pan; shallow-fry pork, in batches, until browned both sides and cooked through. Drain on absorbent paper.
Slice pork and serve topped with ginger; serve tonkatsu sauce separately.
tonkatsu sauce combine ingredients in small bowl; mix well.

serves 4
per serving 33.7g fat; 2953kJ (706 cal)
tip use pork fillets in this recipe if you prefer; stale breadcrumbs and english mustard can be used if you are unable to find the japanese version.

sukiyaki

400g fresh gelatinous noodles (shirataki), drained
8 fresh shiitake mushrooms
600g beef rump steak
4 green onions, sliced thinly
300g spinach, trimmed, chopped coarsely
125g can bamboo shoots, drained
200g firm tofu, cut into 2cm cubes
4 eggs

broth
1 cup (250ml) japanese soy sauce
½ cup (125ml) sake
½ cup (125ml) mirin
½ cup (125ml) water
½ cup (110g) caster sugar

Make broth.
Rinse noodles under hot water, drain. Cut noodles into 15cm lengths.
Remove and discard mushroom stems; cut a cross in the top of caps.
Trim beef of all fat; slice thinly. Retain a small piece of beef fat for greasing the sukiyaki pan. Arrange ingredients on platters or in bowls. Place broth in medium bowl. Break eggs into individual bowls; beat lightly.
Heat greased sukiyaki pan (or electric frying pan) on a portable gas cooker at the table; add quarter of the beef, stir-fry until partly cooked. Add a quarter of each of the vegetables, tofu, noodles and broth. To serve, dip cooked ingredients in egg before eating. As ingredients and broth are eaten, add remaining ingredients and broth to pan, in batches.
broth combine ingredients in a medium saucepan; cook over medium heat, stirring, until sugar dissolves.

serves 4
per serving 36.7g fat; 3921kJ (938 cal).

yakitori

1kg chicken breast fillets
¼ cup (60ml) mirin
½ cup (125ml) light soy sauce
⅓ cup (80ml) sake
2cm piece fresh ginger (10g), grated
2 cloves garlic, crushed
¼ teaspoon ground black pepper
1 tablespoon sugar

Cut chicken into 2cm pieces.
Combine chicken with remaining ingredients in large bowl. Refrigerate
30 minutes. Drain chicken over small bowl; reserve marinade.
Thread chicken onto 12 bamboo skewers. Cook skewers on heated oiled
grill plate (or grill or barbecue), turning and brushing with reserved marinade
occasionally. Cook until yakitori are browned all over and cooked through.

serves 4
per serving 13.8g fat; 1614kJ (386 cal)
tip soak bamboo skewers in water for at least 1 hour before using to avoid
scorching and splintering during cooking.

seared tuna with chilled soba

200g soba
¼ cup (60ml) mirin
2 tablespoons kecap manis
1 tablespoon sake
2 teaspoons white sugar
5cm piece fresh ginger (25g), grated
1 clove garlic, crushed
4 tuna steaks (800g)
1 sheet toasted seaweed (yaki-nori), sliced thinly
2 green onions, chopped finely
1 teaspoon sesame oil
2 tablespoons pink pickled ginger, sliced thinly

Cook soba in large saucepan of boiling water, uncovered, until just tender;
drain. Rinse under cold water; drain. Place in medium bowl, cover;
refrigerate until required.
Meanwhile, combine mirin, kecap manis, sake, sugar, fresh ginger and
garlic in small jug.
Cook fish in heated lightly oiled large frying pan, uncovered, until cooked
as desired (do not overcook as tuna has a tendency to dry out). Add mirin
mixture to pan; coat fish both sides in mixture. Remove fish from pan; cover
to keep warm.
Bring mixture in pan to a boil, then reduce heat; simmer, uncovered,
30 seconds. Strain sauce into small jug.
Meanwhile, place seaweed, onion, oil and pickled ginger in bowl with
soba; toss gently to combine. Divide fish among plates, drizzle with sauce;
top with soba. Serve with wasabi, if desired.

serves 4
per serving 13.2g fat; 2182kJ (522 cal)

lobster and soba
with ponzu dressing

2 small carrots (140g)
½ small daikon (200g)
4 green onions
200g green tea soba
4 cooked lobster tails (660g)
1 sheet toasted seaweed (yaki-nori), shredded finely

ponzu dressing
2 tablespoons mirin
2 tablespoons japanese soy sauce
1 teaspoon sugar
1 teaspoon wasabi paste
½ teaspoon sesame oil

Using vegetable peeler, slice carrots and daikon lengthways into ribbons;
cut ribbons in half lengthways. Cut green onions into 10cm lengths; cut
each piece in half lengthways. Place vegetables in large bowl of iced water;
refrigerate 30 minutes.
Make ponzu dressing.
Cook soba in large saucepan of boiling water, uncovered, until just tender;
drain. Rinse under cold water; drain. Place soba in large bowl; toss gently
with three-quarters of the dressing.
Cut lobster tails in half lengthways; remove vein. Divide drained vegetables
among serving plates; top with soba and lobster tails, drizzle with remaining
dressing, sprinkle with seaweed.
ponzu dressing combine ingredients in screw-top jar; shake well.

serves 4
per serving 2.7g fat; 1411kJ (337 cal)

tempura prawn salad

2cm piece fresh ginger (10g), chopped coarsely
¼ cup (60ml) soy sauce
¼ cup (60ml) mirin
1 tablespoon caster sugar
3 lebanese cucumbers (390g)
2 tablespoons pink pickled ginger, sliced thinly
1 small red onion (100g), halved, sliced thinly
100g mizuna
32 uncooked medium king prawns (1.5kg)
vegetable oil, for deep-frying

tempura batter
1 egg, beaten lightly
½ cup (75g) cornflour
½ cup (75g) plain flour
¾ cup (180ml) iced soda water
32 uncooked medium king prawns (1.5kg)
vegetable oil, for deep-frying

Press fresh ginger through garlic crusher into screw-top jar; add sauce, mirin and sugar, shake dressing until sugar dissolves.
Using vegetable peeler, slice cucumbers lengthways into thin strips. Place cucumber and pickled ginger in large bowl with onion and mizuna; toss gently to combine.
Shell and devein prawns, leaving tails intact. Heat oil in wok or large saucepan; dip prawns in batter, one at a time, draining excess. Deep-fry prawns, in batches, until browned lightly; drain on absorbent paper.
Pour half of the dressing over salad; toss gently to combine. Divide salad among serving plates; top with prawns, drizzle with remaining dressing.
tempura batter combine egg, flours and soda water in medium bowl, mixing lightly until just combined. Do not overmix, mixture should be lumpy. Stand 5 minutes.

serves 4
per serving 18.5g fat; 2243kJ (536 cal)

spinach with roasted sesame seed dressing

⅓ cup (50g) sesame seeds
1 teaspoon sugar
1½ tablespoons japanese soy sauce
¼ cup (60ml) primary dashi (see page 25)
600g spinach, trimmed

Toast seeds in a heated dry small frying pan, stirring constantly, until seeds brown lightly and begin to pop. Reserve 1 teaspoon of seeds; blend, process or grind remaining hot seeds until smooth. Combine ground seeds with sugar, sauce and dashi in a screw-top jar; shake well until sugar dissolves.

Bring medium saucepan of water to a boil, immerse spinach 30 seconds; drain immediately. Rinse under cold running water; drain.

Gently squeeze out excess water; place on serving plate.

Just before serving, pour dressing over spinach. Serve at room temperature, sprinkled with reserved sesame seeds.

serves 4
per serving 7.4g fat; 472kJ (113 cal)
tip you could use tahini (sesame seed paste) instead of grinding the toasted sesame seeds.

sushi salad

2 cups (400g) koshihikari rice
2 cups (500ml) water
2 lebanese cucumbers (260g)
½ small daikon (200g)
1 lemon, unpeeled, quartered, sliced thinly
400g piece sashimi salmon, sliced thinly
¼ cup (35g) toasted sesame seeds
1 sheet toasted seaweed (yaki-nori), shredded finely

mirin and wasabi dressing
4cm piece fresh ginger (20g), grated
2 tablespoons mirin
1 teaspoon wasabi paste
1 tablespoon soy sauce
⅓ cup (80ml) water
¼ cup (60ml) rice wine vinegar

Rinse rice in strainer under cold water until water runs clear. Place drained rice and the water in medium saucepan, cover tightly; bring to a boil. Reduce heat; simmer, covered tightly, on low heat, about 12 minutes or until water is absorbed and rice is just cooked. Remove from heat; stand rice, covered, 10 minutes.

Meanwhile, make mirin and wasabi dressing.

Using vegetable peeler, slice cucumbers lengthways into ribbons. Slice daikon thinly; cut slices into matchstick-sized pieces. Combine rice, cucumber and daikon in large bowl with lemon, fish, dressing and half of the seeds; toss gently to combine. Divide salad among serving bowls; top with seaweed and remaining seeds.

mirin and wasabi dressing place ingredients in screw-top jar; shake well.

serves 4
per serving 13.3g fat; 3078kJ (735 cal)

glossary

bamboo shoots young shoots of certain species of bamboo; they have a mild flavour. Available in cans; drain before use.

bean sprouts also known as bean shoots; tender new growths of beans and seeds germinated for consumption as sprouts. The most readily available are mung bean, soy bean, alfalfa and snow pea sprouts.

chinese cabbage also known as peking or napa cabbage, wong bok or petsai. Elongated with pale green crinkly leaves.

daikon a type of long white giant radish, also known as mooli. Used raw or cooked; also common in pickles.

dashi powder powdered form of dashi, the essential Japanese base stock. Made from kombu (kelp) and dried bonito (a type of tuna) flakes, dashi forms the base for many dishes, including miso soup, stews, noodle soups and salad dressings.

dried thick udon Thick, white wheat-flour noodles available in various widths and fresh and dried forms.

dried wheat noodles many types and thicknesses of wheat noodle are used in Japan: udon are thick and chewy; somen are very fine noodles; hiyamugi are somewhere in between. Some types are eaten cold during summer.

firm tofu also known as bean curd; off-white, custard-like product made from "milk" of crushed soy beans. It is valued for its high protein content. It may be firm or soft depending on how long it has been pressed.

fresh gelatinous noodles (shirataki) thin vermicelli made from a glutinous, yam-like tuber called devil's tongue. They come in both dried and fresh forms.

green onion also known as scallion. It is a young onion, picked before the bulb has formed, having a long bright green edible stalk.

green tea soba buckwheat noodles flavoured with green tea; eaten hot or cold.

gyoza or gow gee wrappers small thin squares or rounds made of wheat flour, used for wrapping dumplings.

japanese mint (shiso) leaves. Also known as perilla, and a member of the mint family; the leaves look more like nettles. Of the two types, one is eaten fresh, the other used in pickles.

japanese mustard a very hot yellow mustard, similar to english mustard. Use it sparingly.

japanese soy sauce a seasoning that is made of soybeans, wheat and salt. It is naturally brewed. The artificially brewed and coloured Chinese versions are best not used as substitutes.

kecap manis a dark, thick, sweet, spiced soy sauce; widely used in South East Asian cuisines. Use as a dipping sauce, condiment, ingredient or marinade.

koshihikari rice the premium rice of Japan, distinguished by its aroma, sweet flavour and sticky texture, and used for sushi.

lebanese cucumber thin-skinned type of cucumber with sweet flesh and small or no seeds when young.

light soy sauce this type of soy sauce is paler in colour than dark soy sauce, but contains more salt. Light soy sauce is used when you don't want to darken food too much.

mirin a pale gold spirit-based rice liquid, also known as as sweet rice wine. Made for cooking, not drinking, and used in sauces, dressings and stews.

mizuna a large-leafed herb with a slight peppery mustard flavour, used in salads and some stews.

primary dashi dashi is a stock base made from kombu (also konbu) which is dried kelp, and flakes of dried bonito (katsuobushi). The first simmering of the ingredients produces primary dashi; if the solids are re-used, they produce secondary dashi.

ramen the name given both to soup stock with various toppings and to noodles.

red cabbage a variety of ball cabbage with distinctive purple-red leaves.

red miso paste one of many types of fermented soybean paste used in soups and stews. Generally, the darker the miso, the saltier and denser it is.

red wine vinegar fairly mild, flavoursome vinegar made from red wine exposed to a bacterial souring process; used in salad dressings.

rice vinegar made from vinegar and a natural rice extract, rice vinegar is less sharp than other vinegars. Japanese rice vinegar has a milder, sweeter flavour than other rice vinegars.

rice wine (see sake)

packaged japanese breadcrumbs also known as panko, these large, sweetish dried breadcrumbs are used to coat fried foods.

pink pickled ginger thinly sliced fresh, young ginger; pickling turns it pale pink. It is served as a condiment and accompaniment to rich foods such as sashimi, which uses fatty fish, or to deep-fried foods.

pork butterfly steaks a pork chop with bone removed, sliced down its length without cutting all the way through, then flattened out to form a butterfly shape.

sake an alcoholic liquid made from fermented cooked rice. It has a clean, dry flavour, and comes in various grades for either drinking or marinating and as part of dipping sauces. Can be served warmed or chilled.

seasoned fried bean curd skins thin pouches made of bean curd, used for stuffing with rice or cut into strips and added to soups and sautéed dishes.

seaweed used in soups and stews. Also used in the form of paper-thin sheets (nori), pressed and dried, which are used to wrap sushi, or shredded as a condiment.

sesame seeds black and white are the most common; there are also red and brown varieties. A good source of calcium, the seeds are used in cuisines the world over. To toast, spread the seeds in a heavy-based frying pan; toast briefly over low heat.

sesame oil strongly flavoured oil extracted from toasted sesame seeds; may be infused with chilli.

seven-spice mix (shichimi togarishi) made from seeds and seaweed and seven ground spices. Togarishi, a hot red japanese pepper, is the only one always included in the mix; the other ingredients are variable but may include mustard seeds, nori (seaweed) flakes, poppy seeds, sansho pepper, sesame seeds and shiso.

shiitake mushrooms a strongly flavoured mushroom available both fresh and dried.

smoked dried bonito flakes (katsuobushi) shavings of dried, smoked and cured bonito, a type of tuna. The large flakes are used for making stock (dashi); smaller flakes are used as a garnish.

soba soba noodles are grey-brown and made from buckwheat flour. They are available in fresh and dried forms, and can be served hot or cold.

sukiyaki sauce commercial sauce containing soy sauce, sake, sugar and dashi stock. It is used in sukiyaki, a one-pot meal comprising beef and vegetables.

sweet chilli sauce a thick, sweet, sticky, hot sauce of red chillies, vinegar, sugar and garlic.

tonkatsu sauce thick sauce, similar to steak sauce and worcestershire sauce, used as a dipping sauce for deep-fried pork.

wasabi paste a hot, pungent condiment that is made from the root of the japanese wasabi plant.

white vinegar a colourless vinegar used in pickling for cosmetic reasons rather than for its flavour.

index

conversion chart

MEASURES

One Australian metric measuring cup holds approximately 250ml, one Australian metric tablespoon holds 20ml, one Australian metric teaspoon holds 5ml.

The difference between one country's measuring cups and another's is within a two- or three-teaspoon variance, and will not affect your cooking results. North America, New Zealand and the United Kingdom use a 15ml tablespoon.

All cup and spoon measurements are level. The most accurate way of measuring dry ingredients is to weigh them. When measuring liquids, use a clear glass or plastic jug with the metric markings.

We use large eggs with an average weight of 60g.

DRY MEASURES

METRIC	IMPERIAL
15g	½oz
30g	1oz
60g	2oz
90g	3oz
125g	4oz (¼lb)
155g	5oz
185g	6oz
220g	7oz
250g	8oz (½lb)
280g	9oz
315g	10oz
345g	11oz
375g	12oz (¾lb)
410g	13oz
440g	14oz
470g	15oz
500g	16oz (1lb)
750g	24oz (1½lb)
1kg	32oz (2lb)

LIQUID MEASURES

METRIC	IMPERIAL
30ml	1 fluid oz
60ml	2 fluid oz
100ml	3 fluid oz
125ml	4 fluid oz
150ml	5 fluid oz (¼ pint/1 gill)
190ml	6 fluid oz
250ml	8 fluid oz
300ml	10 fluid oz (½ pint)
500ml	16 fluid oz
600ml	20 fluid oz (1 pint)
1000ml (1 litre)	1¾ pints

LENGTH MEASURES

METRIC	IMPERIAL
3mm	⅛in
6mm	¼in
1cm	½in
2cm	¾in
2.5cm	1in
5cm	2in
6cm	2½in
8cm	3in
10cm	4in
13cm	5in
15cm	6in
18cm	7in
20cm	8in
23cm	9in
25cm	10in
28cm	11in
30cm	12in (1ft)

OVEN TEMPERATURES

These oven temperatures are only a guide for conventional ovens. For fan-forced ovens, check the manufacturer's manual.

	°C (CELSIUS)	°F (FAHRENHEIT)	GAS MARK
Very slow	120	250	½
Slow	150	275 – 300	1 – 2
Moderately slow	160	325	3
Moderate	180	350 – 375	4 – 5
Moderately hot	200	400	6
Hot	220	425 – 450	7 – 8
Very hot	240	475	9

Are you missing some of the world's favourite cookbooks?

The Australian Women's Weekly cookbooks are available from bookshops, cookshops, supermarkets and other stores all over the world. You can also buy direct from the publisher, using the order form below.

MINI SERIES £3.50 190x138MM 64 PAGES

TITLE	QTY	TITLE	QTY	TITLE	QTY
4 Fast Ingredients		Dried Fruit & Nuts		Party Food	
15-minute Feasts		Drinks		Pasta	
30-minute Meals		Fast Food for Friends		Pickles and Chutneys	
50 Fast Chicken Fillets		Fast Soup		Potatoes	
50 Fast Desserts (Oct 06)		Finger Food		Risotto	
After-work Stir-fries		Gluten-free Cooking		Roast	
Barbecue		Healthy Everyday Food 4 Kids		Salads	
Barbecue Chicken		Ice-creams & Sorbets		Simple Slices	
Barbecued Seafood		Indian Cooking		Simply Seafood	
Biscuits, Brownies & Biscotti		Indonesian Favourites		Skinny Food	
Bites		Italian		Spanish Favourites	
Bowl Food		Italian Favourites		Stir-fries	
Burgers, Rösti & Fritters		Jams & Jellies		Summer Salads	
Cafe Cakes		Japanese Favourites		Tapas, Antipasto & Mezze	
Cafe Food		Kids Party Food		Thai Cooking	
Casseroles		Last-minute Meals		Thai Favourites	
Char-grills & Barbecues		Lebanese Cooking		The Fast Egg	
Cheesecakes, Pavlova & Trifles		Low Fat Fast		The Packed Lunch	
Chinese Favourites		Malaysian Favourites		Vegetarian	
Chocolate Cakes		Mince		Vegetarian Stir-fries	
Christmas Cakes & Puddings		Mince Favourites		Vegie Main Meals	
Cocktails		Muffins		Wok	
Crumbles & Bakes		Noodles		Young Chef	
Curries		Outdoor Eating		TOTAL COST	£

Photocopy and complete coupon below

Name _____

Address _____

_____ Postcode _____

Country _____ Phone (business hours) _____

Email*(optional) _____

By including your email address, you consent to receipt of any email regarding this magazine, and other emails which inform you of ACP's other publications, products, services and events, and to promote third party goods and services you may be interested in.

I enclose my cheque/money order for £ _____ or please charge £ _____

to my: ☐ Access ☐ Mastercard ☐ Visa ☐ Diners Club
PLEASE NOTE: WE DO NOT ACCEPT SWITCH OR ELECTRON CARDS

Card number | | | | | | | | | | | | | | | |

3 digit security code *(found on reverse of card)* _____

Cardholder's
signature _____ Expiry date ____ /____

To order: Mail or fax – photocopy or complete the order form above, and send your credit card details or cheque payable to: Australian Consolidated Press (UK), Moulton Park Business Centre, Red House Road, Moulton Park, Northampton NN3 6AQ, phone (+44) (01) 604 497531, fax (+44) (01) 604 497533, e-mail books@acpmedia.co.uk. Or order online at www.acpuk.com
Non-UK residents: We accept the credit cards listed on the coupon, or cheques, drafts or International Money Orders payable in sterling and drawn on a UK bank. Credit card charges are at the exchange rate current at the time of payment.
All pricing current at time of going to press and subject to change/availability.
Postage and packing UK: Add £1.00 per order plus 25p per book.
Postage and packing overseas: Add £2.00 per order plus 50p per book. **Offer ends 31.12.2007**